Cameron
Goes to
School

**By Sheletta Brundidge
and Lily Coyle**

**Pictures by
Darcy Bell-Myers**

Illustrated by Darcy Bell-Myers
ISBN: 978-1-64343-866-5
Library of Congress Control Number: 2020902754
Printed in Canada
First Printing: 2020

24 23 22 21 20   5 4 3 2 1

Cover and interior design by Darcy Bell-Myers
Written by Sheletta Brundidge and Lily Coyle

Beaver's Pond Press, Inc.
939 Seventh Street West
St Paul, MN 55102
(952) 829-8818
www.BeaversPondPress.com

To order, visit www.ItascaBooks.com
or call (800)-901-3480 x 118
Reseller discounts available.

SHElettaMakesMeLaugh.com

This book is dedicated to Chelsey at the Lovaas
Institute and to Jana at the Family
Achievement Center. Thank you, ladies,
for helping Cameron to find her voice. — S.B.

To all of the moms sending their babies to kindergarten.
You're going to be just fine, I promise. — L.C.

For my daughter, Amelia, and other kids on the
spectrum; embrace your superpowers! — D.B.M.

Everybody says I'm going to school someday and I don't know what to think about that. It's a big change. Especially when you have autism, like I do.

So I just don't
say a thing.

Now they say I'm going to school in one year. Mom is already sad.

"Cameron, when you're there making new friends, who will play Candyland with me over and over again? And again? And again?"

I don't say a thing.
I just study my
ABCs.

Now they say
I'm going to school
next fall. Dad is pretty
broken up about it.

"Cameron, when you're
taking that big yellow bus
back and forth, who will I drive
to all the playdates and lessons
and appointments?"

I don't say a thing. I just work on my numbers.

Now they say I'm going to school at the end of the summer.

Grandma Cynthia is getting nervous. "Cameron, when you're busy learning how to spell and add and write, who's going to decide what TV shows I have to watch?"

I don't say a thing.
I just practice cutting
and pasting.

Now they say I'm going to school in a month.

Big brother Andrew is all put out. "Cameron, when you're off taking field trips, who's going to sneak into my room and mess with all my stuff?"

I don't say a thing. I just memorize all the months of the year.

Now they say I'm going to school in three weeks.

Little brother Daniel is very concerned. "Cameron, when you're there listening to Teacher, who's going to be sitting on Mom's lap right when I want to be sitting on Mom's lap?"

I don't say a thing. I just put my new school supplies in my backpack.

Now they say I'm going to school in ten days.

Mr. Phil, our neighbor, is so worried. "Cameron, when you're out playing games on that big school playground, who's going to leave toys all over my yard and pick my flowers?"

I don't say a thing.
I just work on tying
my new shoes.

Now they say I'm going to school next Tuesday. Chelsey, my therapist, is brokenhearted.

"Cameron, when you're singing songs with your classmates, who will sort through all these flash cards with me?"

I don't say a thing.
I just pick out my
first-day outfit.

Now they say I'm going to school today and everybody's pretty worked up about that.

It's a big change for them.

But I think
they'll be okay.

So I just say,
"Goodbye!"

A Few Good Things to Know about Autism

Autism isn't something that can be caught from another person. Autism is just another way for people's brains to work.

Autism isn't something new. Autism has been around forever.

People on the *autism spectrum* are all different and totally unique. *Spectrum* means all different types of one thing gathered together in order, like all the colors in the world lined up in a rainbow. We say that people are on the *autism spectrum* because people with autism are as different from each other as the colors of the rainbow are different from one another. It might be hard to notice autism in one person while it is easy to notice it in another. If you have autism, you might be super good at drawing pictures while another person with autism might hate drawing pictures. One person with autism might be very, very quiet all the time. Another might not!

Some people with autism can have *ticklish* senses. Our main senses are touch, taste, sight, smell, and hearing. Some of these senses might be almost *ticklish* for people who have autism. For instance, if you have autism, you might be really bothered by a strong smell or a bright light that nobody else seems to notice. Or you might enjoy touching or tasting or hearing something so much that you want to touch, taste, or hear it over and over again.

Some people with autism use *stimming* to feel calm. *Stimming* can be body movements, like tapping, squinting, teeth grinding, hand-waving, or rocking. Stimming can be repeating the same words or sounds. Stimming can also be sorting objects or even chewing or sucking on objects. Most people stim in some small way when they feel nervous or excited. If you have autism you might stim more often, more noticeably, and for longer stretches of time, because it helps you feel calm.

Some people with autism can be very, very interested in certain things. Some people with autism can't get enough of one particular activity or idea. It could be doing math, building with Legos, or decorating cupcakes. Everything else might be *way too boring*, for now.

Some people with autism like routines . . . a lot. A routine is something that always happens at the same time, in the same order, in the same way. If you have autism, a routine—knowing what's coming—might make it easier for you (and for most people) to stay calm and in control.

All people with autism have feelings. Most people who *don't* have autism show their feelings on their faces or in the tone of their voices. If you have autism, you might have the same expression on your face or the same tone in your voice much of the time, because your feelings come out in other ways. Instead of smiles or frowns, you might rather use words to express your feelings or to learn other people's feelings. Whether you have autism or not, try saying "I'm sad" when you feel sad. Ask someone else how they're feeling if you're unsure about it.

All people with autism can be friends with people who don't have autism. People with autism can play games and go to birthday parties and get jobs and start families and do the usual things that people do. If you have autism, you might sometimes act in ways that make it seem like you'd rather be alone, but that doesn't mean you can't or shouldn't be part of the group. Join if you want to join! And if you know someone with autism, invite them to your party or to play in your game!